Business Etiquette & Protocol

Professional Development Series

Contributing Author:
Carole Bennett, Ed.D.
Santa Rosa Junior College
Santa Rosa, CA

D0967359

SOUTH-WESTERN

TM

THOMSON LEARNING

Australia • Canada • Mexico • Singapore • Spain • United Kingdom • United States

SOUTH-WESTERN

THOMSON LEARNING

Business Etiquette & Protocol
By Carole Bennett, Ed.D.

Executive Editor:
Karen Schmohe

Project Manager:
Dr. Inell Bolls

Editor:
Carol Spencer

Marketing Manager:
Chris McNamee

Marketing Coordinator:
Cira Brown

Production Manager:
Jane Congdon

Manufacturing Manager:
Carol Chase

Art and Design Coordinator:
Michelle Kunkler, Darren Wright

Cover and Internal Design:
Grannan Graphic Design, Ltd.

Compositor:
Electro-Publishing

Printer:
R.R. Donnelley/Crawfordsville

For more information, contact South-Western Educational Publishing
5101 Madison Road
Cincinnati, OH 45227-1490.
Or, visit our Internet site at
www.swep.com.

For permission to use material from this text or product, contact us by
Phone: 1-800-730-2214,
Fax: 1-800-730-2215, or
www.thomsonrights.com.

Enhance Your Professionalism . . .

Business Etiquette and Protocol, part of the Professional Development Series from South-Western, will focus on the basics of business etiquette, dining and entertainment etiquette, and international etiquette and protocol. You will learn how to operate in various environments and how to handle etiquette and protocol issues in a practical and responsible manner.

EXPLORE these other professional resources available from South-Western! Continue down the path of higher achievement by sharpening the professional skills necessary for success in the today's high-speed business environment.

The 10-Hour Series

This series enables you to become proficient in a variety of technical skills in only a short amount of time through ten quick and easy lessons.

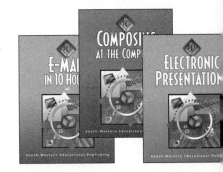

0-538-69458-0	E-mail in 10 Hours
0-538-68928-5	Composing at the Computer
0-538-69849-7	Electronic Business Presentations

Quick Skills Series

Quickly sharpen the interpersonal skills you need for job success and professional development with the Quick Skills Series. This series features career-related scenarios for relevant and real application of skills.

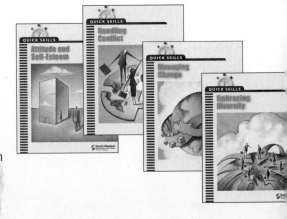

0-538-69026-7	Attitude and Self Esteem
0-538-69833-0	Handling Conflict
0-538-69839-X	Managing Change
0-538-69842-X	Embracing Diversity

SOUTH-WESTERN
™
THOMSON LEARNING

Join us on the Internet
www.swep.com

Contents

Preface

Today's business professionals are moving in an ever-faster society. We are having to learn more at a faster rate than ever before. We are accepting new challenges and new roles that those before us never had to do. Technology has enabled us to communicate faster and to be more productive as a society than ever before thought possible. Along the way, however, we may be a bit guilty of overlooking our manners—especially as they relate to business and professional etiquette. Welcome to *Business Etiquette and Protocol*, a module that presents both general and business manners acceptable in the United States.

Message to the User

Business Etiquette and Protocol has been organized into nine key topics for easy reference. Several case studies are listed at the end of the module. When finished with this module, place it along with your other valuable references. You will return to it many times during your career.

Features

Each topic begins with clear goals entitled "At the Core." A list of key concepts learned is presented at the end of each topic. A pre- and post-assessment activity also is included at the beginning and end of the module; it may be used as a fun, nongraded activity. Throughout the module, in "On the Scene," the author provides firsthand stories relevant to the issues discussed.

About the Author

Carole Bennett, Ed.D., has years of experience in the business and educational fields. She spent a year traveling the nation as a professional seminar speaker. As a worldwide traveler, she was able to observe social skills of leaders in the business world, in the public-service sector, and in the academic community locally, nationally, and internationally.

Her teaching experience includes over 20 years at the college, university, and high school levels. Most recently, she has taught business courses at Santa Rosa Junior College in northern California. Additionally, she has been a business owner and an active leader in the Santa Rosa Chamber of Commerce and the local community. She completed her doctoral degree in education at the University of San Francisco.

Pre-Assessment Activity

Directions: For each item listed below, CIRCLE THE NUMBER that most accurately describes your actions and attitudes for that question. There are seven possible choices for each item:

Never	Almost Never	Seldom	Sometimes	Usually	Almost Always	Always
1	2	3	4	5	6	7

THERE ARE NO RIGHT OR WRONG ANSWERS. There also is no time limit, but you should work as rapidly as possible. Please respond to every item on the list.

Items: *Never*   *Always*

1. I know most rules of etiquette, and I know when
   I am purposely breaking a rule.   1 2 3 4 5 6 7

2. I am comfortable walking down a sidewalk with
   my colleagues—both men and women.   1 2 3 4 5 6 7

3. I feel as though my clothes are "business professional"
   for my particular work environment.   1 2 3 4 5 6 7

4. I am very comfortable with small talk
   at a business function.   1 2 3 4 5 6 7

5. I am comfortable introducing people,
   especially those at work.   1 2 3 4 5 6 7

6. I am pleased to shake hands with whomever I am
   being introduced—men and women, young and old.   1 2 3 4 5 6 7

7. I am familiar with what rules of etiquette to follow
   at the workplace.   1 2 3 4 5 6 7

8. I know how to organize and facilitate a meeting so
   that I respect everyone in attendance.   1 2 3 4 5 6 7

9. I am very comfortable eating a meal in the presence
   of higher-level employees at work.   1 2 3 4 5 6 7

10. I am very comfortable when it comes time to decide
    who is to pay the restaurant tab.   1 2 3 4 5 6 7

11. I am aware of the misperceptions that international
    visitors may have of Americans, which then helps me
    adjust my behavior.   1 2 3 4 5 6 7

12. I am comfortable speaking with international visitors.   1 2 3 4 5 6 7

13. I am comfortable with my knowledge of how to
    display the U.S. flag.   1 2 3 4 5 6 7

Business Etiquette: The Basics

The first rule of etiquette is that the other person feels comfortable. This applies to all settings and social situations. The way for all of us to feel more comfortable in any type of corporate environment is to understand and have a pragmatic knowledge of basic business etiquette. Once we know the rules of etiquette and are comfortable using them, we can make our own choices regarding their application. We can gain a level of confidence knowing the basic rules of etiquette. This level of confidence transfers to our ability to relate to all kinds of business environments. This confidence also enhances our value as individuals as well as our value as employers and employees. We will begin by discussing common courtesy outside the office environment.

Opening Office Doors

First of all, consider opening doors. If you are a woman and a man wants to open the door for you, allow him to do so. Consider it a gesture of courtesy to you as another person. Do not think of it as an act that is condescending. In contrast, however, if you are a man and a woman wants to open the door, allow her to do so. Consider it a gesture of assertiveness in the business world rather than one of gender assertiveness. Traditionally a man opens the door for a woman, an elder, or a senior in authority. A woman traditionally opens a door for either an elder or a senior in authority.

ON THE SCENE

I recently worked for a female CEO whose actions revealed the unexpected. The female CEO expected the door to be opened for her by anyone who walked with her, whether it was a man or a woman. Additionally, if she arrived at the door first, she opened it and walked through it first.

As a woman, slow your gait as you approach a door. When walking with a man who is older, give him a comfortable opportunity to open the door. If he doesn't, just open it yourself. When walking with people your age or younger, take turns opening the doors for each other as you progress through a building.

As a man, make an attempt to open the door for a woman, an elder, or a person of senior authority. Do not make a big show of it, however. If you are a man, think ahead and try to position yourself to open the door easily. Consider the individuals involved and the cultural environment. And remember that common courtesy is genderless.

©Digital Vision

TIP Try to be comfortable with others no matter how they act, and try to make others comfortable in your presence. This is the etiquette rule that is paramount over all others.

Opening Car Doors

Traditionally men open car doors for women, and men do the driving. However, these are not the roles observed in the business world today. Often women do the driving, and there are both men and women passengers. It is correct for the driver (the one with the keys) to at least unlock the passenger door before walking around to the driver's side. If the driver is a man, he should first open the door for the passengers. If the driver is a woman, she also can open the passenger door prior to walking to the driver's side.

Newer vehicles with remote door-unlocking devices almost make this issue moot. Sometimes passengers are not aware that all doors are unlocked, and they patiently wait for the door to be opened. A courtesy might be to announce that all the doors are unlocked.

If it is raining, the driver (whether man or woman) should offer to walk to the car and drive it back to where the sheltered passengers are waiting. In this case, the driver should unlock all the doors before arriving for the passengers. If two equivalent individuals go together in a car, the passenger should not consider it rude to have to wait while the driver opens his or her door first then unlocks the passenger door from the inside.

Walking on Sidewalks

Traditional etiquette rules state that when walking on a sidewalk, the man always walks on the outside, or curbside, of a woman. Many mature men still feel more comfortable walking on the outside. The traditional rule was developed when streets were muddy and vehicles often splashed mud onto individuals walking down the street. The gallant man was supposed to take the brunt of the mess. Today's fast-paced business climate does not always expect this traditional rule to be followed. People walk together down a sidewalk without much regard for positioning.

Today's police departments and self-defense classes teach us that the common threats or dangers to a pedestrian in contemporary society are in and around the dark alcoves of buildings. Using that logic, a man today should walk on the inside of the sidewalk (away from the curb), thus protecting a woman from a would-be assailant.

Giving Up Seats

©Digital Vision

If you are riding public transit or seated in a waiting room with limited seating, be conscious of those around you. If someone appears less fit than you, be polite and offer him or her your seat. Someone less fit might include an older person, a person who appears out of breath or tired, a person who does not have good balance inside a moving vehicle (bus), a person burdened with parcels, or a person who appears to be disabled. It is common courtesy for both men and women to give up their seats if the situation presents itself.

If you are standing and someone offers you a seat and you feel it is not justified, simply say "Thank you, but I'm fine. Perhaps someone else would like to sit down."

ON THE SCENE

In a large meeting room with a shortage of chairs, it is appropriate for a woman wearing pants to give up her seat for another woman wearing a skirt or dress. Obviously, it would be easier for me as a woman in pants to sit on the floor or stairs. Common sense is usually synonymous with common courtesy.

The Corporate Culture

A recent tour of Cisco Systems, a large and fast-growing high-tech corporation, revealed a diverse nature of employees. In the employee cafeteria, there were men and women of different ethnicities and ages. To further the diversification, a few employees were dressed rather conservatively, yet most were dressed in casual work attire.

Most of the time we adapt quite readily to a working environment. There are times, however, when employees are asked to represent their company in a foreign or unfamiliar environment. Representing oneself or one's company in an unfamiliar business environment can present some challenges. Sometimes local habits and customs cause others to be uncomfortable, focusing attention on the "insiders" and excluding the "outsiders." In the way a formal environment can make us feel uncomfortable, a less-formal environment can make us feel uneasy.

> **TIP** There is a big difference between those individuals who break the rules and know they are breaking them versus those who break the rules and do not know they are breaking them. The big difference is awareness, which means the ability to be comfortable in almost any environment. Being comfortable means being confident.

Therefore, the rationale for taking this course is to be aware of and understand the correct rules of business etiquette. Whether you choose to follow them or not is your decision. Confidence comes with being cognizant of the rules and making conscious decisions whether or not to adhere to them.

Manners are Cost Effective

More than just allowing you to gain personal confidence, "good manners are cost effective. They increase the quality of life in the workplace, contribute to optimum employee morale, embellish the company image, and hence play a major role in generating profit. On the other hand, negative behavior, whether based on selfishness, carelessness, or ignorance, can cost a person a promotion, even a job."[1]

"Up to 90 percent of unhappy customers never complain about discourtesy, and up to 91 percent will never again do business with the company that offended them. In addition, the average unhappy customer will tell the story to at least nine other people, and 13 percent of unhappy customers will tell more than twenty people."[2]

Typically, a round dining table at a conference might serve eight to ten people. It can be almost humorous—and definitely predictable—to watch the anxiety developing on the faces of a few people around the table. Everyone is seated at approximately the same time. The panic sets in when people look at the overwhelming number of eating utensils, glasses, and plates in front of them. Adrift on a sea of silverware, they do not know which belongs to them or where to begin. It is fun to watch the eyes of the people around the table. Some have an air of confidence and know exactly what to do. Others sit anxiously with their hands in their laps waiting for someone else to make the first move. Actually, this is a smart thing to do if you are not sure of yourself. But think about how much more confident you could be if you knew exactly what to do. People gain a new level of respect for their "socially aware" colleagues who act with an air of confident ease at a social setting in the business world.

Try imagining what goes through the minds of people in such settings. They might be thinking, "Oh, my gosh! I know my parents used to tell me rules of etiquette, but I never thought I would have to remember to use them. I should have listened to what they were saying!"

We are moving up the corporate ladder because of our intelligence, our talent, and our creative abilities. Admittedly, we are a bit rusty when it comes to business etiquette.

©Digital Vision

TIP Keep in mind that there is a vast difference between those who break the rules through choice and those who break the rules through ignorance. It shows!

Competitive Edge

Corporate America is a fast-moving culture, and competition is an inherent factor. Corporations and businesses compete, and divisions within corporations compete against each other. Departments within divisions compete, and individuals within departments are competitive. Having knowledge of business etiquette can be one more tool to provide you with a competitive edge over others. It can be *the* tool that gives you the promotion you well deserve.

Repeatedly there are stories of individuals who have not been hired or who have not been promoted because of an inadvertent social *faux pas*. They may never have received feedback that an etiquette error was their problem. They may never have known why they were overlooked for the position. Could this ever have happened to you? Think about this question as you work your way through the module.

Perception Is Essential

Think about the individuals who seem to know exactly what to do and when to do it and are always able to execute it with grace and style. Whether you like them or not, don't you secretly admire them? Don't you tend to think they probably have attended some special training program that you have not had access to?

Remember that correct behavior is learned behavior. If you commit yourself to practice the information in this module, you can generate the perception that you also have had that special training program. Practice in all settings, especially the most comfortable settings (such as at home), so that proper etiquette will become second nature to you in the work environment.

> **TIP** Knowing standard business etiquette means that you know what to do, when to do it, and how to do it with grace and style.

RECAP OF KEY CONCEPTS

- The first rule of etiquette is that the other person feels comfortable.
- Knowing the rules of etiquette helps builds confidence, which can improve competition in the business world.
- Traditionally a man walks on the outside of a sidewalk, a man drives the car, and a man opens the doors; these roles have changed with today's business climate.
- Positive behavior reflecting good manners to others is cost effective for business.

Corporate Dress and Presentation

AT THE CORE

This topic examines:

> ➤ **TODAY'S CORPORATE ATTIRE**
> ➤ **HOW TO TREAT CLIENTS AND/OR VISITORS COURTEOUSLY**
> ➤ **THE USE OF EFFECTIVE EYE CONTACT WITH OTHERS**
> ➤ **THE EFFECT THAT SMILING HAS ON OTHERS**
> ➤ **THE IMPORTANCE OF LEAVING AN EMPLOYER WITH A POSITIVE FEELING**

There is a general statement "You never have a second chance to make a first impression." How you package yourself and present yourself to the public is important to you personally for career advancement; it is also important to your employer and to the image of the company.

Dress and Presentation

There was a plethora of books written in the 1980s about dressing for success—both for men and women. The "uniform" for success was at its peak during that time. This section will explore today's attitudes toward professional dress.

There has been a quiet rebellion against the dress-for-success rigidity within many corporations, especially in the high-tech world. Today's clothing guidelines are definitely more relaxed. However, there are still some basic rules. Remember that the way you dress reflects your personal marketing strategy; it is your "packaging." Many corporations have changed to "business casual," which consists of comfortable clothes that could be considered "dress casual."

courtesy of ©PhotoDisc, Inc.

The first rule, no matter where you work, is to learn the corporate climate. Basically, be alert. What are your bosses wearing? What is the attire of those employees who have gained a great deal of respect? A general guide is to wear clothes that are somewhat similar to those who are one step above you. You can dress for the job you want while dressing appropriately for the job you have.

General Guidelines for Dress and Presentation:

Rule: Do not mix styles. If one day you are dressing with a preppy look, then be consistently preppy from head to toe. If you are dressing with a European look, then be consistent with that look, too.

Rule: If you are color blind, get help. Have retail salespeople help you coordinate your clothes; then organize them in your closet so you remember what goes together. You do not need to make a fashion statement—just be sure your clothes and accessories match.

Rule: Avoid clothing that is too tight. Buy your clothes just a bit larger than you need to, to present a more flowing and stylish look. This is especially true for men's shirts and women's blouses.

Rule: Keep your shoes in good condition. Nothing ruins a "look" like unpolished shoes, run down heels, or holey soles. Unkempt shoes can detract from one's overall appearance.

Rule: Keep jewelry simple. In the business environment, modesty is the general rule with jewelry. If you wear three sets of earrings in each ear at home, wear just one pair to the office.

Rule: Avoid risqué clothing. It is not appropriate for the office. This is true for both men and women. It is unprofessional to see a man's chest, biceps, or belly peeking out from a shirt. Likewise, it is totally unprofessional to see a woman's cleavage or bare shoulders or too much bare leg. It may get attention—but not the kind of attention for long-term professional respect. Leave some aspects of your personal life (like overly casual or revealing attire) separate from your work life.

courtesy of ©PhotoDisc, Inc.

Casual Days

If your job requires you to dress casually on designated days, then do so. But remember that your professionalism needs to transcend your casual attire. If you deal directly with the public, try to maintain the image you project every other day—customers appreciate it. If you plan to go somewhere after work that requires more casual attire, bring clothes and change at the end of the day.

Office Visitors

When someone takes the time to come to your office to see you, give your whole attention to that person. Make solid eye contact. Do not shuffle papers or talk on the telephone. If you are busy, say so.

©Digital Vision

You do not have to give away your precious time to visitors, however. There are ways to control your time. For example, while glancing at the clock, say "I've got an appointment at 2 p.m., so I have about four minutes for a quick chat. What's going on?" Then give your undivided attention. Make people feel welcome. Outside visitors should never be considered an interruption of your work.

If you are in a service organization (which probably applies to most workers), consider everyone who comes your way to be a potential customer. You should never be too busy to share a kind word, to give quick directions, or to answer a question.

If a talkative coworker comes by, stand up when that person arrives, and stay standing. Do not invite him or her to sit down. Say "Where are you headed this morning? I'll walk in that direction with you." Then walk together out of the building, go in separate directions, and return alone.

Eye Contact

©Digital Vision

Depending on the size of the community, there is a big difference in how strangers make eye contact. In big cities, strangers rarely make eye contact with others in public. Conversely, in small towns, you are expected to make eye contact with strangers on the street. In fact, you would be considered rude if you did not also smile and say "Good morning," "Hello," or at least "Hi."

If you live in a small town and visit large cities, you may have to remind yourself to curtail your customary small-town friendliness. You want to appear confident and alert, but people might misinterpret your intentions.

Direct eye contact between professionals is considered excellent business practice. Older traditional manners encouraged women *not* to make direct eye contact. In today's American business culture, however, eye contact is a positive means of projecting confidence, honesty, and good intentions. Lack of direct eye contact (especially in conversations between two people) can be offensive or perceived as deceitful.

ON THE SCENE

During a recent networking reception at a conference, I was feeling very uncomfortable. Whenever I started a conversation, the person with whom I was speaking would look over my shoulder. I had the impression the person was looking for someone else to talk to (obviously someone who was more important than I). I know this is just perception, but it does not leave a good impression. I am always impressed when someone of authority takes time to give me his or her undivided attention. I am especially impressed when I know there may be many others around who also want to talk to this person and that my partner in conversation is not distracted. The benefit of habitually giving your undivided attention is that you will earn the reputation of being a good listener.

Smile

We all know how wonderful it is to have someone smile at us, and this is especially true in the work environment. A simple smile can positively enhance your work environment by altering a negative mood, nurturing camaraderie, and reinforcing self-esteem.

Smile when you see people. Smile when you meet people. Smile when you talk to people. Smile even when you talk to people on the telephone. Did you know that people actually *hear* a smile?

ON THE SCENE

In a former job, I passed rows of office workers on the way to my office. I always made a point to smile and acknowledge them personally as members of our work team. One day a woman I barely knew came into my office. "Do you have a minute?" she said. "I want you to know how much I appreciate working around you. You've been so pleasant and uplifting. I've been going through some personally trying times. The only nice part of my day has been coming to work and seeing your lovely smile. I've always wanted to thank you for helping me through this difficult time." This experience taught me that you never know how your attitude might affect another person. One courteous act communicates volumes.

Leaving a Job

When you plan to leave a place of employment, be pleasant during your remaining time. No matter how you feel, do not "bad mouth" the place of employment. You never know when your bad actions will come back to haunt you. Remember that these are the people who provided you with a paycheck.

When you apply for a job, reference checks will be made. People talk to people they know; they do not call just the people you have listed on the application. It is amazing what you can learn about people in casual conversation. "Hey, Tom. You used to work for XYZ, didn't you? I thought so. Did you ever know someone named Susan Jones who worked in data processing?" That's how the *real* reference checks happen. Often people don't even realize they are supplying a reference check when they take part in such a conversation.

ON THE SCENE

Recently, I left a fabulous job. The people I left actually felt hurt and rejected. I could feel it when I informed them I was leaving. "Didn't you enjoy your job? What did we do to make you want to leave?" Such responses made me feel I had to give a reason for my departure. I made sure I expressed my sadness in leaving and that my decision was based on the necessity to live closer to my family and on my desire to return to teaching.

RECAP OF KEY CONCEPTS

- One of the basic rules of appropriate professional attire is to learn the corporate climate.
- When someone comes to your work area, give him or her your undivided attention so he or she feels welcome.
- Eye contact between the listener and the one who is talking is necessary for effective communication.
- Smile when you see people; it is contagious.
- If you plan to leave a place of employment, do not talk negatively about your employer or the company's product or service; doing so could come back to haunt you.

Interacting with People

uality management practices recognize that all people are our "clients." Outside visitors to our company, of course, are potential clients, but people within our own organization should also be considered our clients.

Making Introductions

When you introduce two people, look first to the person you consider to be more important. Say that person's name first, followed by "I would like you to meet…" Then look at the person being introduced, and reverse the order. How you make the introductions of people infers who you consider to be more important.

It helps to add a pertinent comment about the person to get the conversation going. Note in the following examples how the brief comments are added to the end of each introductory line. This provides a starting point for conversation between the individuals being introduced.

Introducing your boss to your visiting sister: "Dr. Smith, I would like you to meet my sister Jan Edwards, who is going to have lunch with me today. Jan, this is the president of our college, Dr. Marie Smith."

When individuals appear to be fairly equal in authority, you can choose who is "more special." If your guest, for instance, is a personal friend who is visiting you at work, you would probably begin with Joe Howard, the vice president: "Mr. Howard, I'd like you to meet my friend Carla Miller, who is going to lunch with me today. Carla, this is Joe Howard, our vice president." However, if you were providing a tour of the company to a special guest, you might chose to begin with him: "Carla, I'd like you to meet our vice president, Joe Howard. Joe, this is Carla Miller. She's my special guest today from Intel® Corporation and is touring our facility."

courtesy of ©PhotoDisc, Inc.

Introducing a younger person to an older person: "Mrs. Alomar, I want you to meet Bill Bromwell, who is responsible for organizing the event today. Bill, this is Mrs. Alomar; she's an active member of our Foundation."

Repeating Names

As soon as someone has been introduced to you, make an attempt to repeat his or her name. This is a technique reinforced by Dale Carnegie[3] in his books and nationally recognized seminars and has been taught to salespersons for years. The other person feels recognized when you repeat his or her name. Additionally, repeating the name helps you better remember it. Here are some examples:

- "Exactly how do you spell your last name, John?"
- "I have a cousin who also has the name Barbara."
- "Dr. Mason, where do you live?"
- "Senator Barberi, would you like some refreshments?"
- "The name Hans sounds German. Is it?"

Forgetting Names

When meeting a lot of people on a daily basis, it can be difficult to remember names. However, some people are offended if you don't remember their names.

I have often moved to new communities, changed careers, and changed work environments. Each time a change is made, I must become acquainted with hundreds of new faces. For the person who stays in one job for, say, 40 years, the difficulty of remembering all those new faces may go unappreciated. It is easier being in one place and learning just the names of a few new people over the course of time.

Be tolerant of people who are new to your environment. Try hard to remember others' names, but do not be harsh if others cannot remember yours. Some people will use nicknames rather than real names: "Hi, buddy." "Hello, partner." "Hey, friend." This may be a way to get by if they do not remember names very well. The friendliness of the greeting is at least a start.

It may be better to be honest if you cannot remember someone's name. Say something such as, "I can't believe it! I've gone blank again. Please tell me your name one more time."

Shaking Hands

Shaking hands is very much an American custom. If you are not comfortable shaking hands, you are missing a wonderful opportunity to connect with other people.

Take time to practice shaking hands with a few close friends. Ask them what your handshake feels like. Practice until you have a firm "vertical" handshake. In other words, don't turn your knuckles, forcing the other person to give a "curtsy" handshake. Your hands should meet on an equal basis. Men should not shake hands with a woman any differently than they would with another man.

A handshake should not be a bone crusher, keeping in mind that a person wearing

courtsey of ©PhotoDisc, Inc.

rings may feel pain if a handshake is too strong. Conversely, a handshake should not be limp. Some people are offended by a limp handshake, as the perception is one of being frail. People prefer a firm, friendly handshake.

When you know you are going to be introduced to others, be sure your right hand is free. If you are a woman, carry a bag over your shoulder. If you are at a social event, carry your plate or glass with your left hand so your right hand is free.

Three shakes seem to be about right. A lingering handshake is not necessary. Letting go prematurely, however, may indicate you are not comfortable with the person. Rely on your best sense of social timing.

When meeting someone new, try waiting for the other person to release your hand first. This might appear trivial, but you can tell he or she, appreciates it (along with, of course, a nice smile and direct eye contact).

If you are at work sitting behind your desk or on the other side of a table when a visitor comes by, walk around your desk so you are next to your visitor when you shake hands. This effort shows a sincere interest on your part in greeting the other person.

The days of women staying seated while men shake hands are long gone. In the business environment, all people should stand, recognize each other, and shake hands with each other. Women who are uncomfortable with this role should practice being more assertive and shaking hands until they become more comfortable.

Making Small Talk

Some people dread social events because they are uncomfortable with small talk. You do not have to be a victim. You can learn to take control of conversation. You can make a social situation as interesting as you want it to be.

One of the big secrets to good conversation is to ask questions. Learn to ask questions that are open-ended, not closed. A closed question is one that begs only a one-word response. Here are some examples of dead-end closed questions that do nothing to enhance good conversation.

- "How are you today?"
- "Are you having a good time?"
- "Did you come in the same vehicle as the Browns?"
- "Which class did you decide to take for your staff development requirement?"

Do you get the idea? The short answers, respectively, would be as follows:

- "Fine, thank you."
- "Yes."
- "No, I came with Alice."
- "The Internet class."

If you seek information asking open-ended questions, you will get more meaningful answers. You actually will be able to lead conversations. You will not have to do much of the talking unless you want to, and you will learn a great deal about other people. Here are examples of open-ended questions to use when asking for information.

- "Tell me about the highlight of your day."
- "Who have you talked to, and what did you learn?"
- "How did you get here?"
- "What have you learned in the course you chose to take for staff development?"

If you ask questions like these, you will have lively verbal interaction that will be of interest to you and the other person. In addition, people will think you are the life of the party. Try it.

The Art of Conversation

At social gatherings, people are generally most comfortable around people they know. They will group together, appearing to exclude others. The intent is not to be exclusive, but an outsider or new person may find it a challenge to join into conversation with such an established group. In this section, we will explore techniques you can use to reach out to new people.

Entering a Room. A room full of people can be a daunting experience if you do not have a plan of action. Preparing a plan before you enter a room will give you more confidence than just wandering into the room and hoping for the best.

First, consider what you want to accomplish, and focus on that. Are you there to celebrate a friend's achievement? Are you there to network and meet new people? Are you there to see friends and perhaps meet a couple of new people? Are you there to meet the love of your life? Again, keep the focus on why you are there. Set realistic goals, so they will be easier to accomplish. Making six new friends may not be too realistic. It may be easier to meet one new person with whom you have something in common. You will feel a sense of accomplishment and not be too disappointed in yourself if you set realistic goals.

Next, settle yourself and gain a sense of the whole room. After you first enter, stand off to one side, and survey the room. Breathe deeply a few times, and gain your composure. Check for people you recognize; then continue surveying the room. Look for interesting people you may want to meet. If you do find some people you know, walk over to them and acknowledge them, but do not stay with them the entire time. Make a point of getting to know new people. Keep in mind your original plan.

Starting a Conversation. Do not expect people to come up to you and begin a conversation. If you do, you may be alone for quite a while. Look for someone who is also alone. It is much easier to walk up to an individual and start a conversation than it is to walk up to a group of people. Find an individual who is not with anyone and start your conversation there.

Introduce yourself to the person. "Hello. My name is ... What's yours?" Offer your hand in greeting. Give a little information about yourself; then ask some questions to start the conversation. Prepare ahead of time, especially if you are shy. Here are some suggested comments with open-ended questions.

- "I'm new here and don't know anybody. Do you know any of these people?"
- "I'm a bit shy when it comes to these kinds of things. What usually happens?"

- "This is my first time to one of these events. Have you attended before? What's is it like?"

- "I believe I saw you at the last meeting. What did you think of it?"

- "I'm a new hire as of last week. What do you do here at the company?"

- "I'm here at the wedding from out of town. How do you know the bride and groom?"

ON THE SCENE

When I first moved to the community of Santa Rosa, California, I knew only a few people. I attended one of my first parties at a private residence, but none of the few people I knew had arrived yet. I had no one to talk to. I saw a man off by himself, leaning next to the refrigerator. I began asking him some open-ended questions. He beamed when I began making conversation with him, and we both enjoyed our conversation off to the side of the crowd. I later learned that I had been talking to Charles Shultz, the creator of Peanuts, who was known to be a shy person and not one comfortable with conversation. We established an acquaintance that continued for years.

In the book *How to Start a Conversation and Make Friends*[4], the authors suggest that you remember the acronym *SOFTEN*, which will remind you of certain actions to take.

- Smile
- Open posture
- Forward lean of your body
- Touch with a nice handshake
- Eye contact
- Nod in affirmation

A genuine smile with a twinkle in your eye is a powerful way to communicate your willingness to meet another person. Just smile and say "hello." You will have someone to talk to in no time at all.

Negative body language can turn people away as quickly as a smile can engage them. Slouching, folding arms over your body, or leaning with legs crossed are all considered negative, or closed, postures. On the other hand, standing is always more approachable than sitting. Standing tall with an alert posture is positive. Plant both feet on the ground, supporting yourself in an upright manner. Communicate to others by your body language that you are willing to be engaged in conversation.

When you begin a conversation with another person, lean forward slightly toward the person. Tilting your head forward provides the same gesture. Consider people from Japan, who actually bend at the waist and bow when meeting someone. Americans nod slightly or lean forward, which may be a holdover from days gone by of bowing and curtsies. The reverse of this is to lean backward or lift the chin, which communicates the notion of being repulsed by someone.

Keeping Promises

Do not trust your memory. Have a follow-up system ready so you remember to keep the promises you make. Carry a note pad, for instance, so you can write down even the smallest commitment you make.

You actually provide a compliment to people and impress them when you remember seemingly unimportant things. "Norman, here's that article on Harley-Davidson® I was telling to you about." "Sonja, here's my doctor's name and phone number I promised to share with you." "Joe, here's that web site we were talking about."

Use the calendar program on your computer to make notes to yourself. "Marie goes to Washington tomorrow. Call to see if she needs anything." "Henry's mother has surgery today. Send her a card." "Al's daughter graduates with an M.A. degree next week. Buy her a gift." You will be perceived as a compassionate person if you reach out to people and remember special events in their lives. Your awareness (and thoughtfulness) will work to your advantage.

Exchanging Business Cards

Having personal business card enables you to network with people in the business world. You can exchange business cards at professional meetings and other events where you practice your conversation skills.

Your personal business card should have all pertinent information — your name, address, and phone number. Items such as e-mail address, fax number, logo, or motto are helpful additions. If you do not yet have a job or if you work out of your home, you may want to think twice about putting your home address on a business card. Consider obtaining a post office box for your official address. Or your phone number and e-mail address may be sufficient. Be sure the card is not cluttered and looks professional.

Artville™

Microsoft Publisher® has an easy-to-follow Wizard that takes you through the process of designing a business card. Many formats are available that will give your card a professional appearance. You can buy plain business card stock from a stationery store to use in printing out your cards. At first, print just one page of ten cards. Hand out some cards to people, and observe their reactions. Evaluate the information on the card before printing more. Ask your friends and colleagues for their input. Your business card is a personal statement, so you want it to be right.

After meeting new people and talking with them, you may want to ask for their business cards. Then you can politely ask "Would you care to have my business card?" But keep in mind that exchanging business cards should follow a conversation of some substance.

Organize the business cards you collect from people. You may want to jot a few notes directly on the card that will jog your memory later. (For example, "He is interested in talking to me after I graduate.")

RECAP OF KEY CONCEPTS

- When introducing one person to another, take into consideration who the "senior" person is or the one of higher rank; that is the person to whom the other person should be presented.

- When introducing someone, include a sentence about the person that will invite conversation between the two people being introduced.

- When you are introduced to someone, repeat that person's name as soon as possible so it will be easier to remember.

- An American handshake is firm but not crushing; combine it with sincere conversation.

- Small talk is more interesting if you use open-ended questions that invite more than one-word responses as answers.

- Conversation can be aided greatly if you have a plan of action before entering a room.

- Carry a pen and paper to write notes to yourself so you can follow up on any promises you make.

- Always carry a professional business card ready to exchange with others at a business networking event.

———◇———

Office Etiquette

➤ **MODEL BEHAVIORS THAT SHOW RESPECT TO YOUR EMPLOYER AND CO-WORKERS**

➤ **TACTFUL WAYS TO OVERCOME UNCOMFORTABLE OFFICE SITUATIONS**

➤ **HOW TO COMPLAIN TO A SUPERIOR AND GIVE A MEANINGFUL SOLUTION OVER WHICH YOU HAVE CONTROL**

➤ **HOW TO LEAVE EFFICIENT AND EFFECTIVE TELEPHONE MESSAGES**

To give your work life the quality of your personal life, you need to apply many of the same energies and skills. Be punctual. Be discreet. Empathize. Offer privacy. See the big picture. Dress to match the occasion. Behave honorably. The Golden Rule finds no better expression than in the workplace.

The Work Day

Managers become annoyed with employees who appear to watch the clock. Managers especially resent those who spend 15 or 20 minutes preparing to leave for the day. These same people are the ones who arrive on time, yet spend 15 or 20 minutes getting ready to start their work day. If your day begins at 8:30 a.m., you should be in the office (with your coat hung up and your coffee poured) at your desk at 8:30. Likewise, if your day ends at 5 p.m., then 5 p.m. is the time to begin packing up your belongings for your departure. If you have an hour for lunch, that does not mean you leave 15 minutes before the hour and return 15 minutes after the hour. Keep in mind that you are being paid to work a certain number of hours. You owe it to your employer to give that amount of time in actual work.

©EyeWire

If you are a salaried employee, you have more of an obligation to accomplish your assignments. In American culture, salaried persons often work more hours during the week than the office staff, including the lunch break. Actually, lunch is an excellent time to accomplish a good deal of work. At lunch, you are away from the usual interruptions. The pleasant atmosphere in a restaurant sets a different mood. If you are in a position to do work during lunch, take a pad of paper so you can jot down notes or plan strategies.

Take time to have lunch with all of your coworkers — people you work with at all levels. About 15 minutes before lunch, walk into an office and say "Anybody here who does not have lunch plans? I don't have any plans today and would love to join someone." Even if you receive no offers (and feel a bit rejected), you will have spread some good will around the office.

Respecting Others

There is a motto that says "Everyone needs and deserves to be treated with dignity and respect." This does make sense. Make sure you treat everyone at your workplace with respect.

You often spend more hours of your "awake life" with those at work than you do with members of your own family. This should make you stop and consider how many times a day you choose to criticize rather than empathize. It is important to nurture your relationships at work, as they can be vitally important to your personal happiness. There are ways to sustain a positive and healthy working relationship with your coworkers. First, treat everyone with respect.

ON THE SCENE

I know an office assistant who rolls her eyes and uses a contemptuous tone when speaking of her boss in his absence. If someone is looking for him and he happens to be at a meeting, she says "Who knows where he is? It's after 3, and he's rarely here this late." Instead, she should say, "You missed him again. He's so busy with various meetings that I can hardly keep up with him. Let me have your number so he can call you for an appointment."

Try to avoid the habit of using possessive pronouns when describing coworkers. For example, instead of saying "This is *my* assistant Mary," say "This is Mary who works in the Research Department." Another version would be "This is Mary who works with me in the Research Department." Leave it to Mary to explain her role and what she does. After all, the two of you are working together for the same end.

Making or Not Making Coffee

Making coffee for the boss is frequently perceived as a demeaning chore for an assistant. Bosses may think that since they are paying the salary, they should be able to ask their staff to do anything. The whole issue comes down to courtesy and respect for each other.

The task of making coffee can be shared, which makes it much less demeaning. For instance, a boss can say to an administrative assistant, "Toni, I'm going down to the staff lounge. Would you like a cup of fresh coffee?" Toni will be more amenable later when her boss asks "This afternoon I'm having some special guests come into the office. Would you mind bringing us coffee then? I sure would appreciate it."

"Not in My Job Description"

One of the most annoying sentences in the workplace is "That's not in my job description." Employers cringe when they hear employees say those words or express the attitude behind the words.

Many offices today follow quality management practices. With this in mind, the customer (client, student, patient) deserves the utmost respect. Everyone should try to accommodate the customer's needs. Many times that customer is internal. For instance, a manager can be the customer to the Payroll Department.

As employees, we should consider how we can all work together to get the job done as well as to provide the utmost service to our clients. Even if we are asked to do something outside of our job description, we should never respond with the sentence "It's not in my job description." Instead, we could say "I'm not the most knowledgeable person on that subject. Michael has more experience. Let me take you over to his office." Or "You really need to be talking to Joanna, who's in charge of our employee fitness program. Let me give her a ring and see if she's available."

Complaining Effectively

Most managers spend a good portion of their time solving problems. This part of their job may not be pleasant. It is certainly important to be honest about job concerns, especially those that affect productivity and overall effectiveness. A healthy way to complain, however, is to be as objective as possible and present realistic solutions over which you can be directly responsible.

Do not just register a complaint: "I have a real problem with Fred's unwillingness to do work outside of what he considers his job description."

Do not bother to register a complaint accompanied by a solution over which you have no control: "I have a real problem with Fred's unwillingness to do work outside of what he considers his job description. Why don't you tell him that he should change his attitude."

Do register a complaint with a solution over which you have some control: "I have a real problem with Fred's unwillingness to do work outside of what he considers his job description. I was wondering if both he and I could attend the upcoming quality workshop. I'd be glad to be his study partner. Maybe he'll open up more with his self-imposed job parameters."

Making Others Look Good

Try to give away more credit than you feel is actually due. Some people may not agree with this, but in the long run, you will be rewarded for doing so.

If coworkers contribute on a project, put their names in print as participants. When giving a speech, say "And we couldn't have accomplished this project without all the help provided by..." In actuality, their input may have been quite limited. So what. They will always appreciate the fact that you mentioned their names.

Workers resent an individual who takes credit for a project on which he or she had barely any input. People will be glad to work on your team knowing that you do not take all the credit yourself and that you share it with others.

Try to support the decisions of others, especially if you are working in a participatory decision-making environment. If a team works together to make a decision that isn't exactly in line with your thinking, support the decision anyway. As long as the decision is not life threatening or totally misguided, go along with it. Support it and think of the long-term picture of developing a productive team of co-workers.

Telephone

Organizations spend an incredible amount of money on marketing to gain the attention of potential clients. The first point of contact for most new clients is a telephone call. This is the first impression a potential client will have of your company.

If you are in a position to answer telephones for your organization, consider how important it is to make a good impression.

When you answer the telephone, identify yourself using your first and last name. Identifying yourself properly saves time and confusion. Generally, it is unprofessional in many situations to identify yourself only by your first name. Women are particularly guilty of this. "Health Center, this is Kay."

©Digital Vision

ON THE SCENE

I do not think some of my friends realize how frustrating it is when they call my voice mail and say "This is Bill. I need to schedule a meeting. Call me back." I must know at least seven different men named Bill!

When using the telephone, don't forget to smile. People actually hear a smile! Your tone of voice on the telephone sets the tone of the business transaction to follow. Answer every telephone call as if it were the first one of the day, and there is a million dollars pending that call!

Professional use of the telephone includes returning calls. Not returning telephone calls sends a negative message. If you don't actually want to talk to an individual, call when he or she will not be available (such as during the lunch hour) and leave a message. At least you will have returned the call.

Leaving Messages

Almost everyone today has voice mail. Do not get into the "loop" of playing telephone tag. Try to be as succinct as possible. Give some idea of why you are calling, and leave any pertinent information. Often business can be taken care of by leaving a quick message. You can eliminate hours of wasted time by becoming a practiced message leaver and receiver.

An example might be "Hello. This is Keisha Jaders in the Accounting Department. There appears to be an error on your purchase order #0137 for the scanner you ordered. The quantity is two, but the price total is for three items. Could you please clarify this? My extension is 4473." This is a much better way to use voice mail than saying, "Hello. This is Keisha Jaders. Please call me on extension 4473. It's urgent."

And the answer to this problem probably can be solved with one quick reply on the telephone, perhaps to Keisha's voice mail.

Slow down when leaving your telephone number. Many people leave a very clear message but speed up when they get to their phone number. Remember to slow down.

Getting Attention

An old sales trick works well when you are calling busy people. Ask, "Do you have a minute?" A positive response to the question commits them psychologically to focus on your telephone call. "Hi, Jose. I'm glad I caught you. I need to talk to you about our annual budget. Do you have a minute?"

It does work. People then focus on what you have to say even if they have a distraction at hand. They have made the commitment to listen to you.

Ending the Telephone Conversation

End your conversation on a positive note whether in person or on the phone. Leave people thinking positive thoughts about you as you sign off. Force yourself, if necessary, to think of something positive to say to others. This list of sentences can be used when ending a meeting or telephone call.

- "I always enjoy talking with you; you're so enthusiastic."
- "I always enjoy working with you; you're such a visionary person."
- "I always enjoy our conversation; you keep me very well informed about changes that are taking place."
- "Thank you for the information; you're such an upbeat and pleasant person."

RECAP OF KEY CONCEPTS

- ◆ Business etiquette means being respectful of your employer by working the number of hours for which you are paid.
- ◆ Treat everyone with dignity and respect.
- ◆ Provide the best service possible to customers and clients; do not be guilty of saying "That's not in my job description."
- ◆ If you have a complaint about someone or something, offer it along with a solution over which you have some control.
- ◆ Give others more credit that you think they deserve; you will generally be rewarded for it later.
- ◆ Always answer the telephone with a smile; answer each telephone call as if it were of the utmost importance.
- ◆ Leave telephone messages with some substance so people will not get caught in a telephone message "loop."

———◇———

Meetings

➤ **HOW TO SEND EFFECTIVE INVITATIONS TO MEETINGS**

➤ **HOW TO FACILITATE AN EFFECTIVE MEETING**

➤ **HOW TO DESIGN WAYS TO REWARD PUNCTUALITY**

➤ **HOW TO THANK INDIVIDUALS FOR THEIR ATTENDANCE**

 eetings are an integral part of the business environment. Approximately 25 to 35 percent of a lower-level managers' time is spent in meetings, whereas as much as 50 percent of upper-level executives' time is spent in meetings. Because time is money, meetings are costly to business. Therefore, it is important that the time be spent productively.

Meetings

Meetings vary from a small group of two or three people in an office to several people in a conference room to a large group of people in a hall or an auditorium. You may be involved in one of the stages of organizing a meeting. Knowing how to organize a meeting will enable you to do so with ease and style. Further, by being aware of the protocol of meetings, you can ensure that everyone's time will be spent productively.

When planning a meeting, consider the following:

✔ What date and time is convenient to most people?
✔ Who are the essential people who must attend?
✔ Who are the not-so-essential people who must attend?
✔ Is the facility available at that date and time?

✔ Will refreshments be necessary? Who will provide them?

✔ What kind of audiovisual equipment is necessary? overhead? flip chart?

✔ What are the key items for the agenda?

Invitations/RSVP

If you are having a meeting, a luncheon, or another event, send out invitations so that people receive them in time to plan for the event. (Give them at least two weeks if possible.) An invitation can be an e-mail message, a written memo, or even a telephone call. Double-check all the details before you distribute the invitations. It can be embarrassing when an invitation goes out for an event on Tuesday, May 6, when in fact May 6 is a Wednesday. People become confused and may get the impression you are not very organized.

©DigitalVision

One way to check meeting details is to remember the 5 Ws. Does the invitation tell who, what, where, why, and when? Does your invitation tell *who* is invited? Does it give an agenda or a comment saying *what* will be covered? Does it say *where* the event will take place? Does it say *why* the meeting is to take place? And does it state *when* the meeting will start and end? Further, does it include necessary details about accessing the event, such as parking permits, visitors' passes, and directions?

Attendees like to know ahead of time who has been invited to a meeting. It is easy to indicate the invited individuals at the top of the invitation or memo. You may not be listing them by name, but you can list them by job function (i.e., "To all department heads").

RSVP is an abbreviation of the French phrase "Répondez s'il vous plaît." The English translation is "Please respond." The letters *RSVP* do not create a verb. Frequently we hear the phrase "Have you RSVP'd yet?" A more refined and knowledgeable way to use the letters in a sentence would be "You've received an invitation noting RSVP. Have you responded yet?" When you reply, you might say "I received an invitation. I do plan to attend."

Facilitating a Meeting

No matter how simple a meeting is, an agenda is imperative. An agenda informs the meeting participants of what to expect. Even with an informal meeting, an effective business procedure is to start the meeting by saying "The purpose of this meeting is to cover X, Y, and Z. Is there anything else anyone wants to cover? Okay. Let's start discussing subject X."

In a more formal meeting, an agenda should identify four items for each topic:

1. The subject
2. The person expected to speak on the issue
3. The expected outcome
4. The time expected to cover the topic

Identifying those expected to speak on a topic enables everyone to be prepared, which makes for a productive meeting.

©EyeWire

Describing the expected outcome is essential so everyone knows why he or she is there. Examples of suggested outcomes are discussion only, consensus vote, identification of group leaders, and information only.

The time expected to be spent on a topic enables the meeting leader to say "We've spent enough time on this topic; we need to move on. We can discuss this further at our next meeting." This prevents extremely talkative people from dominating a meeting and keeps a meeting from becoming derailed from its intended purpose.

Rewarding Punctuality

People appreciate other people who arrive on time. Do not reward latecomers by holding up the meeting until they arrive. Begin the meeting on time, thereby rewarding punctuality. When people realize you start your meetings on time, they will make the extra effort to arrive promptly.

Start each meeting with a special bit of worthwhile information (for example, information for them to become a more savvy employee). You can creatively encourage punctuality in your work environment by utilizing time management skills in your meetings.

ON THE SCENE

When teaching business courses at the college, I emphasize punctuality as a positive work trait. I begin exactly on the hour and give extra input on an upcoming test, a tip for success as a student, a job lead, or other "inside" information.

Running a Meeting

Many good management books go into detail on the subject of meetings. If you stress business etiquette when running your meetings, you will win compliments and run productive meetings.

- *The Administration and Conduct of Corporate Meetings*[5]
- *The Art of Successful Meetings*[6]
- *Better Business Meetings*[7]

Agree on the Agenda. No matter how informal your agenda is, the first items on the agenda should be to get all participants to agree on the topics. Ask participants if anything else should be added or deleted. Agreement on the agenda means the participants will stick to the agenda. Adjustments to the agenda can be made as the meeting progresses, but the meeting participants should agree to any changes that are made.

Stay on the Topic. As a meeting leader, if you have a clear agenda, you can keep everyone on track about the topic being addressed. You might say "We're getting off the intended topic. I'd like to propose that we write this down as a side bar item. It's a good topic, and I don't want to lose it. But let's set it aside for awhile and come back to it if we have time at the end of the meeting. If not, it will be on next week's agenda."

A *side bar* is a list of topics that become important but are not on the current agenda. Its purpose is not to forget them. You can keep participants content by adding their topics to the side bar list. They know the topic will be addressed if there is time at the end of the meeting, or the topic will appear on a future agenda.

Using a side bar is also a way to verbally edit people who have a tendency to be long-winded and to dominate meetings with their personal agenda items. For example, you can say "Pedro (the long-winded person), would you mind preparing a quick summary of the facts on that topic for our next meeting. That way we'll all be better informed and ready to discuss it." Then write the topic on your side bar.

Seating Arrangement. Do not sit directly across the table from someone you see as an opponent. Subconsciously it is a direct challenge. Position yourself to the side to be less threatening to the person.

Consider the Cost. When you are at a meeting some time, try this exercise. Count the number of people in attendance, estimate the hourly wage of each person, and add up the numbers. If the meeting is two hours in length, double the cost. Add the preparation time of the person running the meeting, thereby arriving at the approximate cost of the meeting. It is shocking to realize how much time and money is spent.

For example, if a meeting of ten people lasts an hour and each person earns approximately $20 per hour, this one-hour meeting cost the organization at least $200. And most meetings are more expensive than this.

Are meetings really necessary? Always ask yourself

1. Do we really need the meeting?
2. Am I inviting only the people who need to be here?
3. Can I be more efficient in running the meeting?
4. Can some of the agenda items be handled through e-mail, by memo, or by phone rather than holding a meeting?

Sending a Thank-You

Thank-You Notes. If appropriate to the occasion, send a thank-you note. A regular business meeting would not require that you send a note unless, perhaps, you were a special guest.

Sending a thank-you note is the proper gesture following a semi-social event. In a business environment, however, do not overdo it. Sending too many thank-you notes might label you as someone who is going overboard to please.

Having been invited to a special event that requires a response (RSVP) is a clue that the event involves a good deal of work by someone. Send a thank-you note following such an event. While at

©EyeWire

the event, ask for a business card from whomever is in charge if you do not have an exact address. The business card provides the necessary information and ensures correct spelling, making the thank-you note easier to write.

Plain note cards are appropriate for thank-you notes. If your company has generic note cards, you can use those. Your host would appreciate a handwritten note saying "Thank you for including me in the celebration of your department's first million dollars. I can tell you put a great deal of work into the event. I thoroughly enjoyed it."

ON THE SCENE

One of my former CEOs would invite 15 employees at a time to come to her office for coffee and a chat. One of those invited was a recent immigrant to the United States. He responded to the invitation's RSVP by calling to say he would be there. In addition, he sent a dozen roses in a crystal vase with a card. Because he was new to the United States, his act was considered "charming" and was deemed acceptable. In fact, some individuals were impressed by his elegance. However, if a person well versed in American customs did something like that, people might find the behavior a little bizarre.

If you do not have any note cards, you can make some quick "thank-you cards" on your computer. Print them on card stock with the name of your department. Leave the inside space blank where you can hand write your personalized note of thanks.

Thank-You Letters. To show appreciation for someone's work ability or for a business event, you would send a letter keyed on letterhead or a memo keyed on interoffice stationery. This kind of thank you might be saved in someone's professional portfolio.

ON THE SCENE

Recently, the district chancellor was a guest on our campus. The staff I worked with did an incredible job of organizing the event. I knew they were handling a stressful task that was beyond their normal job responsibilities. I was extremely appreciative of what they had done, and I sent each of them a complimentary letter.

RECAP OF KEY CONCEPTS

- ◆ Use the 5 Ws to check the proper contents of a meeting invitation: who, what, where, why, and when.
- ◆ Use an agenda for all meetings to identify the topics, who will speak on the topics, the expected outcomes, and the amount of time that will be spent on each topic.
- ◆ Reward punctuality by sharing a special bit of information at the beginning of a meeting that any latecomers will miss.
- ◆ Getting attendees to agree on an agenda before a meeting begins helps ensure the topics will be covered as planned.
- ◆ Extend your appreciation to those who have worked hard to organize and provide an event.

Dining Etiquette

AT THE CORE
This topic examines:

➤ **ARRIVING AT A RESTAURANT**

➤ **IDENTIFYING THE PARTS OF A PLACE SETTING**

➤ **HOW TO ORDER FOODS THAT CAN BE EATEN EASILY DURING A STRESSFUL BUSINESS MEAL**

➤ **KNOWING HOW TO COMMUNICATE SMOOTHLY WITH YOUR FOOD SERVER**

➤ **HOW TO PAY THE TAB TACTFULLY**

A lot of important business is conducted in a food-related environment, so the more familiar you are with the rituals, the better your chance of having made a positive impression.

There are stories about people being interviewed for jobs who are asked to join a group for lunch. How they handle themselves during the meal becomes part of the decision to hire. Has this ever happened to you? Or did you not even know that dining out was part of the evaluation process? Yes, it is important to many jobs that you can handle yourself appropriately in a restaurant.

Arriving at a Restaurant

If possible, call ahead and make a reservation for the meal. Once your group is together at the restaurant, you do not want to stand around waiting for a table to become available.

ON THE SCENE

If individuals in my group are arriving separately, I normally wait at the door for some of them to arrive. Often the host or hostess will ask if I would like to be seated and wait. But I find it unnerving to be the only one sitting at a table waiting for others. Perhaps this is a personal preference, but it shows how important it is to be on time. Someone waiting in an unfamiliar environment can become apprehensive if the event lacks organization.

If someone is waiting for you, you do not want to have to walk through the restaurant searching for the person. Instead, tell the dining room host who you will be meeting. You might say, "I'm meeting a man (describe him) by the name of Omar Vasquez. If he arrives, please let him know I'm here."

If you are running late, call the restaurant. Describe the person you are to meet. Ask the host or hostess to page him or her with the message that you are on your way. Call the restaurant if you are going to be more than ten minutes late.

In most cases, you will wait as a group to be seated. The women go first, followed by the men. Watch the host, as he or she should pull out the most preferred seat for the woman. This is very traditional. If there are several women, the women may defer to a senior woman for the first seat, otherwise the preferred seat will go to the first woman to arrive at the table. If there is not a woman in the group, the first seat pulled out should be deferred to the highest-ranking person.

Given all this traditional information, the reality is that some people have real hang-ups about where they sit in a restaurant. Some people, for instance, do not like having their backs to the door. Others do not want to be looking in a mirror.

If the table is to seat six or more people, you may decide not to sit at either end (or the head) of the table. Sitting at either end may cause you to be left out of conversation. Try to make an excuse to position yourself at the center of the table so you can join conversations at either end.

If at all possible, try to mix people up in general. Try not to have "regular buddies" or people from the same department sitting beside each other. Try to mix women and men at the table. Eating out is an excellent opportunity to get to know new people in a different setting.

Set a purse or bag on the floor or on an empty chair. These items do not belong on the table. If it is a working meal, take out a pen and your necessary papers to place to one side; but your purse, bag, or briefcase should not be placed on the table. The bottom of these items may be dirty therefore; you do not want them near your food.

Cell phones do not belong in a restaurant. If you are expecting a call, disengage the ring in favor of the vibration. Excuse yourself to go outside, to the lobby, or to the restroom to take a call. People do not realize how loudly they speak into a telephone and how rude it is to others attempting to have a pleasant dining experience.

courtesy of ©PhotoDisc, Inc.

The Napkin

The napkin should go in your lap soon after you have been seated. You can keep it folded on your lap during the beverage portion of the meal. In an elegant restaurant, your waiter may come to the table and place the napkin on your lap for you.

Sometimes locating your napkin can be tricky. Often at business conferences, napkins are decoratively placed into cups or wineglasses or placed in some other clever location. Traditionally they are placed at the left of your dinner plate. If they are in some creative place, pay attention to the utensils at your place setting. Once you figure out what your "territory" is according to your place setting, you can easily decide which napkin is yours.

For instance, perhaps the napkins are rolled up and stuck into coffee cups. You know the coffee cup is always to your right, so the napkin in the cup to your right is your napkin.

Place the napkin on your lap with one fold toward your knees. Never take the napkin out to your side and shake it before placing it on your lap. In addition, the napkin is not meant to be tucked in at your neckline to protect your tie or shirt.

With the fold away from your body and towards your knees, you simply pick up the folded edge, bring it to your lips, blot your lips, and return it neatly to your lap. Use just a corner of the napkin.

If you need to leave the table during the meal, place the napkin in your chair. Do not put it on the table. When the meal is over, fold the napkin loosely and leave it on the on the table where your dinner plate was (or leave it to the left of your dinner plate if the plate is still there).

Place Setting

A total of about 1 1/2 feet of space should be in front of you at the table, representing your place setting. In the center is a space for your main plate. To the right is your cup and saucer. Above the cup and saucer are your glasses and stemware. To the left of your plate is a smaller salad plate (if salad is served at the same time as your main course, or entrée). Above the salad plate is a small bread-and-butter plate.

The utensils are situated at your place setting for use in order from outside to inside. Forks are on the left of your dinner plate. The salad fork would be on the outside, indicating it is used first with your salad. The larger fork would be on the inside; it is used with your main course. If you choose not to have a salad, do not use your salad fork. An alert waiter will remove the unused utensils. However, do not depend on your server for help.

Knives and spoons are to the right of your dinner plate. Spoons are on the outside of knives, but still in the order of use. A large soup-spoon may be on the far right outside a smaller teaspoon for your coffee. You may also have a selection of knives. The knife on the far right may be a smaller one to use with your salad. You may have a funny-shaped knife for use with a serving of fish. A serrated knife may have been added if you plan to eat steak.

Generally all silverware is placed in the presumed order of your meal. If you skip any portions of your meal, skip using those utensils as well.

① Napkin	⑤ Bread Knife	⑨ Salad Plate	⑬ Dessert Spoon
② Water Glass	⑥ Soup Dish	⑩ Salad Fork	⑭ Coffee Cup
③ Wine Glass	⑦ Dinner Plate	⑪ Dinner Fork	⑮ Saucer
④ Bread Dish	⑧ Soupspoon	⑫ Dinner Knife	⑯ Teaspoon

You may find more utensils above your dinner plate. A fork or spoon might be placed horizontally here. These utensils are for dessert — if, of course, you eat dessert.

The napkin (or serviette) is generally located to the left of the forks, but it could be placed anywhere. Very formal settings may include items that expand this basic setting. You may have your own salt-and-pepper set. You may have a place card or name plate to designate your seat. You may have a small bread-and-butter knife placed horizontally on your bread-and-butter plate. If you are unsure of how a utensil is used, watch your host or hostess for cues.

The host should be the one to start eating first. (Perhaps the rule was made so that others would know what to do with their utensils!) In restaurants, wait for everyone at the table to be served prior to eating. If you are a guest in someone's home, wait for your host to sit down before you begin eating. However, it is not rude to begin eating first if your host insists.

I often order a special vegetarian meal. In a conference setting, my meal sometimes takes longer to be served than the other meals. When this happens, I insist the others start their meals before their food gets cold. This is an example of knowing the rule — and knowing when to break it.

Ordering from the Menu

Hold a menu so it does not hide you from everyone else at the table. Sometimes people take a large menu and hold it up as if it were a protective shield.

When you have made your selection, close the menu or place it off to the side as a signal to the waiter that you are ready to order. If you do not want to order for awhile, keep the menu open or in front of you; this will indicate to an alert waiter that you are not yet ready to order.

If you have no idea what price range your host may have in mind, try an opening sentence such as "Have you eaten here before? What would you recommend?" Note carefully what he or she recommends. If it sounds good, order it. Or order something very close in price. The item suggested will give you a clue to the price range your host has in mind.

After the host places an order, you can always change your mind. "That sounds good. I think I'd just like some soup and salad as well. You're setting a good example for me to eat more healthfully."

Think carefully as you order. Order foods that are not messy to eat. For example, try to avoid spaghetti, fettuccini, or noodle-type soups when dining out in a business situation. You do not want spaghetti sauce splattered across the front of you at the end of your meal.

Easy food to eat would be mashed potatoes instead of french-fries. Sliced chicken is easier to eat than chicken parts, as picking meat off the bones of chicken with a knife and fork is difficult to do. A fish fillet is easier to eat than shrimp with their tails. Mixed vegetables are easier to eat than artichokes. A mixed green salad is easier to eat than hearts of romaine salad. You get the picture.

Cafeteria Dining

When you pick up your food on a tray and take it to a table yourself, take the plate, napkin, beverage, and utensils off the tray and set your own place setting. Place the empty tray on an empty table near you, or tilt it up next to a wall near you. If and when you need to clear the table, the tray will be handy. Eating directly off your tray was allright when you were in high school but should be avoided in the work environment.

Your Server

Getting the attention of the server (waiter or waitress) sometimes can be a challenge. You can usually get his or her attention by making eye contact or nodding slightly. A quick wave might be necessary, but to be less obvious, keep your hand signal lower than your shoulder. In America, we do not hiss or snap our fingers to attract the server's attention. Whatever method you choose, remember that discretion is of primary importance.

Always talk softly to your server, as if you were sharing a secret. "Would you mind bringing us another fork, please?" You do not have to point out that the tine is bent or that it is dirty or that it dropped on the floor.

Do not hesitate to get advice from your server. "What is the chef's specialty today?" "Do you have any favorites?" "I don't eat cheese or milk products, so what would you recommend for me?"

When food is being brought to your table, make sure space on the table is clear. Your napkin should already be in your lap. Be sure you have not placed a notebook or piece of paper where the food is to be placed. Be sure your water glass is in its proper location so there will be room for the plate of food.

Food is generally served from the left, and beverages are poured from the right. Knowing this ahead of time, you can sit back in your chair to provide as much room as possible for the server. Servers may not be able to present plates from the "proper" side, depending upon the arrangement of the table. The most important thing, however, is to let them do their job.

Do not take the plate from the server in mid air unless you are in an awkward location and the server has asked for your assistance.

Do not push your plate away from you when you are finished. It is the server's job to remove the plates.

Do not stack your plates at the end of the meal. A signal that you have finished your meal is to place the knife and fork in a parallel position across the dinner plate pointing towards the center. Imagine the handles being at the two o'clock position on the plate with the points at the center of the clock.

Paying the Tab

Once you get the attention of your server, make a quick signal as if you were writing on your hand. This will get the message to your server, even across the room. If you suspect it might be awkward deciding who will pay for the meal and if you want to pick up the tab, you can excuse yourself for a few minutes. Taking your charge card with you, locate your server, and tell him or her that you will pay for the meal.

If you are with a group of people and everyone is sharing the cost, round off the tab and divide it equally. Do not sit in a restaurant and squabble over the amount to be paid. Servers do not like to do separate checks for large groups. If you absolutely need a receipt for business purposes, tell your server ahead of time. You may even want to call the restaurant beforehand and ask what the policy is. If you are a woman in the business world, do not expect a man to pay the tab. Pay your part of the bill whenever possible. Frequently men will say "I'll pay this time; you can treat next time." This might just be a courteous way of not letting

courtesy of ©PhotoDisc, Inc.

the situation become awkward. You might bring up the subject before the bill arrives. "Jerry, I want this meal to be my treat, so don't try any of your usual tricks, Okay?" "Pierre, I'd like to have lunch with you on a regular basis. It's only fair that we split it every time. Okay?"

If you are a man (especially a mature man), you may feel awkward with women paying their share. But a business meal is not a date! You are together to discuss business or to develop a business relationship. You are doing the woman a favor by sharing the meal tab. If you always insist on paying the tab, you are upsetting the balance of a mutual business arrangement.

RECAP OF KEY CONCEPTS

- ◆ Be familiar with a restaurant before making reservations for a group; make a reservation so your group does not have to wait.
- ◆ Being familiar with a typical place setting helps you understand dining etiquette.
- ◆ Closing the menu at a restaurant is a sign to an alert waiter that you are ready to order.
- ◆ Try to order foods that are easy to eat when you are at a business function.
- ◆ Pay your fair share for a restaurant meal; allowing others to always pay the tab places you in a compromising position.

Drinking and Eating Etiquette

AT THE CORE

This topic examines:

➤ **HOW TO DRINK BEVERAGES**
➤ **SELECTING FOODS THAT ARE EASY TO EAT IN A BUSINESS SETTING**
➤ **HOW TO CORRECTLY EAT FOOD**

O nce you are situated in the restaurant or eating environment, you are still confronted with how to consume the food properly. Some food items are especially challenging. This section focuses on these troublesome areas.

Drinking Beverages

Try to drink beverages without leaving lip prints on the glass or cup. As you are eating your meal, take the corner of your napkin and touch your lips to remove any food residue; then take a drink from your glass. The same is true for lipstick. Consider blotting your lipstick before sitting down to a meal. (But do not use your napkin.) It is unappealing to leave lipstick marks all over a glass.

It is unprofessional to drink beverages through a straw. Remove the straw from your glass, and tuck it under the edge of your plate.

courtesy of ©PhotoDisc, Inc.

To Drink or Not to Drink. One of the first decisions you have to make in a restaurant setting is what you want to drink. Whether you choose water or an expensive bottle of wine, order what *you* want. Don't be intimidated.

In a business situation, be wary of ordering alcohol. If this is your first time with a group, be especially cautious. With a new group of people, order an alcoholic beverage only if everyone else in the group decides to do so and only if you want one. Even under these conditions, only order one, never a second. You do not want to lose any sense of composure when you are trying to make a good impression.

The effects of alcohol can sneak up on you. The fun of being with a group of coworkers can be intoxicating in itself. Adding too much alcohol can only allow a situation to get out of control.

If you find yourself being pressured to drink an alcoholic beverage when you really do not want to, try this technique. After you have ordered your drink, excuse yourself. Find your waiter or the bartender.

Tell him or her that whenever you order a drink, you want it to be alcohol-free. Provide a tip, if necessary, to be sure it happens. This allows you to keep up with the crowd, but still maintain your dignity.

Serving Champagne. On a special occasion, you may be asked to serve champagne. Keep the bottle as still as possible before opening it. Carefully remove the foil, and unwind the wire. Hold the bottle over a sink or area that will not be a problem if champagne spews out. Take a clean napkin, and loosely cover the top of the bottle. With your fingers on the outside of the napkin, gently work the cork from side to side until it pops out. With the napkin covering the cork, there will be no breakage or injuries from a flying cork.

Take the same napkin and fold it lengthwise to wrap once around the neck of the champagne bottle. To serve champagne, hold the bottle at the neck with your left hand under the folded napkin, and support the bottle from the bottom with your thumb in the hollow. Your fingers of your right hand further support the base of the bottle. Pour slowly keeping in mind the many bubbles that will form if the champagne is fresh.

The Toast. It is customary to offer a quick toast as a signal for people to begin drinking. The standard favorites are good (for example "Cheers!") You might want to think of a special but short toast for the occasion. "Here's to very good friends." "Here's to the success of our new product." When the food arrives and every person at the table is served, it is nice to say "Bon appetit" or "Enjoy your meal."

For more formal events, the person making the toast may need to think about what he or she wants to say. The person hosting the event most likely will be the person offering the toast. The person being celebrated would *not* offer the first toast. At a company function designed to celebrate the employees, a boss might say "I'd like to propose a toast to all of you who have worked so hard to make this company a success." A leader somewhere in the organization might stand next and say "On behalf of all the employees, I'd like to propose a toast to a super boss."

If you are a person being toasted, the appropriate etiquette is to smile humbly and say "Thank you."

Holding a Wine Glass. Holding a wine glass or champagne glass has a rule, too, but one that is somewhat debatable. Etiquette references state that the bowl of a wineglass should be cupped in your hand. In California's wine country, cupping the bowl is definitely a "no-no." People in the wine country know that you do not hold the bowl of the wineglass in hand because it affects the temperature of the wine.

It is considered correct to hold a wineglass by the stem or the base. Wine aficionados will appreciate your respect for the wine. Here is a clear example of knowing the rule — and knowing you are purposely breaking the rule.

Eating Food

Maintaining correct posture while you eat is a sign of good manners. If you slump over your meals, you do not project a good image. Bring the food to your mouth; do not take your mouth to the food.

Do not put your elbows on the table while you eat. Sometimes, though not very often, it is all right to put your elbows on the table when you are not eating. Watch your host, or watch others in your eating environment. Sometimes people take an "elbow break" at the end of the meal.

American-style eating dictates that you eat your food with the fork in the right hand. When you have to cut your food, shift the fork to your left hand, cut the food into a couple of bite-size pieces, set your knife down, and shift the fork back to your right hand to continue eating.

Bring the food (in small bite-sized portions) to your mouth. Always eat with your mouth closed. Do not talk with your mouth full of food. People will understand if you pause before answering a question. If your bites are small, you shouldn't have to pause too long.

In British-style eating, the fork remains in the left hand with the fork tines pointed downward. The knife stays in your right hand and helps adjust the food for the fork. It is not rude to eat in this manner, but it is a little different for most Americans.

Continental-style eating uses the knife and fork in the same manner, but the fork tines point upward. This also is not considered rude, but it is an eating style that is generally difficult for Americans.

courtesy of ©PhotoDisc, Inc.

If you pause while you are eating, never "hook" your fork over the edge of the plate. Keep the fork on the plate. The same is true for your knife. Keep it on the plate with the point tucked under some food.

If you are eating soup and you pause, put the spoon on the plate under the bowl. If you acciden-tally bump the spoon, you will not spatter soup all over you and other diners.

The correct way to eat soup is to dip the spoon away from you. Bring the soup spoon up, and tip the soup into your mouth. Avoid sipping the soup noisily. When you get to the bottom of the bowl, use your opposite hand to tip the bowl slightly away from you,

courtesy of ©PhotoDisc, Inc.

continuing to dip the spoon away from you. Never pick up the bowl and drink from it — unless, of course, you are in a Japanese restaurant, where it is customary to drink the soup from a bowl.

Breaking Bread. Bread comes in various shapes and sizes. If bread is served in a basket sitting on the table, someone must start the basket around. If you are the person nearest the basket, you are the one to start. Reach for the basket, fold back the linen to expose the bread, then pass it to others. Use your left hand, pass across your body to your right, and say "Would you care to start the bread?" or "Would you care for some bread?" Let the other person be the first to take some bread or decline it. If you start the breadbasket, then you should be the last to take any bread.

If the bread is offered to you, you can accept the basket, remove some bread, then pass it along using the same hand as before. Always try to reach across your body using the hand opposite from the direction you are passing to. If you do not want any bread, accept the basket anyway, and pass it to the next person. Again, accept with your right hand, and smoothly shift the basket to your left hand; then pass it to the person on your right.

When removing bread from the basket, do not touch any bread except for the piece you are going to remove. Often a loaf of bread in the basket is only cut partially, requiring you to finish tearing it into pieces. Use the linen in the basket to hold on to the remaining

courtesy of ©PhotoDisc, Inc.

bread as you tear away the portion you want. If there is no linen in the basket, consider using your own napkin (only when fresh and clean, of course) to touch the bread portion you will be leaving behind.

Now that you have the bread in your hand, it goes on your bread-and-butter plate located to the upper left of your dinner plate. When no bread-and-butter plate is available, place the bread on the edge of your dinner plate. In some Italian restaurants, the custom is to put the breadsticks or bread on the tablecloth next to your plate. A quick glance around the restaurant or at your host will give you a clue as to what is customary.

Eating the bread involves more rules. It is considered polite to put a usable lump or pat of butter on your bread-and-butter plate. Tear off a bite-sized piece of bread, butter it, and eat it. Only take pieces of bread to your mouth that will not be returned to the plate.

- Never butter your bread directly from the butter dish going back and forth with your knife to your bread.

- Never butter the entire slice of bread and take bites from a whole slice of bread.

The same is true for rolls. Put some butter on your bread-and-butter plate. Tear off one bite-size piece, butter it, and eat it. There may be unusual bread in the basket. Large sheets of unleavened bread are popular in some restaurants. Use the same general rules for this hard bread by breaking it into smaller edible portions.

ON THE SCENE

Breadsticks can be fun. I think it is better to take a whole bread-stick, and break off one small portion at a time to eat. Once I saw a breadstick about two feet long! I suppose this would be a time to say something clever, such as "May I break bread with you, my friend?" You could also opt to leave a broken stick behind (without touching it, of course).

Eating Unusual Foods

Eating some foods requires extra finesse. Here are a few foods that require a bit of experience so you are comfortable eating them in a business environment.

Cherry Tomatoes. Cherry tomatoes can be messy to eat if they happen to squirt juice as you bite into them. Cut them in half, if possible. If they become too slippery on the plate or if your knife does not have a serrated edge that will cut them easily, you are better off leaving them on your plate.

Artichokes. Artichokes are unfamiliar to many people. They are served with melted butter or a sauce for dipping. You use your fingers to remove one leaf at a time and dip the pulpy thick end of the leaf into the sauce. The next step is to gently pull the meat off the thick end with your teeth. Avoid the meat from high on the leaf; it will taste bitter. Pull the meat off with your bottom teeth by putting the leaf in your mouth so it is curving downward. Discard the leaf in a container provided for that purpose.

After you have pulled off the bigger individual leaves with your fingers, use your knife and fork to pull the tiny leaves off; discard these. Underneath the leaves, you will find some fuzz. Do not eat any of this. Pull the fuzz away from the tastiest part of all — the artichoke heart. Scrape all the fuzz away, and cut the heart into bite-sized pieces. Pick up one morsel at a time with your fork, dip, eat, and then smile.

Shrimp. Shrimp still in its shell is eaten the way most shellfish are eaten. Use your knife and fork. Hold the shrimp with your fork, and cut off the tail. Still holding the shrimp, pull the shrimp out of its shell with your knife. Larger shellfish may require that you use your fingers to hold the shell as you pull the meat out with your fork.

Try to avoid ordering foods that are challenging to eat when you want to make a good impression. Other foods to be avoided are spaghetti, lobster, whole leaf romaine salad, steamed clams, fried chicken, and barbecued ribs.

Disastrous Things That Happen

If food is caught in your teeth, do not use your finger to pick your teeth. Do not use a toothpick in public. If the food is bothering you, excuse yourself and go to the restroom.

If your fingers get food on them, never lick or suck them. Use your napkin.

If you drop a fork or another utensil, pick it up only if it is easy to do so. Try to catch your server's attention and say "Excuse me. We need another fork."

If someone spills something at a nearby table or a server drops some food, ignore it. Continue your conversation as best you can. It is rude to stop and stare. If you can be of assistance, however, do not hesitate to offer. You might say "Here, use my napkin." If you have no assistance to offer, then politely ignore the situation.

If someone at your table spills something, offer your napkin. Then try to get the attention of your server. Once the server is there, let him or her take over. Continue the discussion as calmly as possible. The person who caused the spill is undoubtedly embarrassed. Re-focus the conversation so the person who caused the accident will be more comfortable. If the person apologizes, simply say "Don't worry about it. We've all had something like that happen to us."

RECAP OF KEY CONCEPTS

- Use a napkin before sipping a beverage so you do not leave lip prints on a glass or cup.
- Be extremely cautious about drinking alcoholic beverages in a business setting.
- Plan ahead if an event calls for a formal toast; have something meaningful to say about the person or situation being celebrated.
- Knowing how to eat bread, soup, and unusual foods correctly will give you a feeling of confidence at a business dinner.

International Customs
and Table Manners

AT THE CORE

This topic examines:

➤ PERCEPTIONS OF AMERICANS BY OTHER CULTURES

➤ HOW TO WELCOME INTERNATIONAL VISITORS

➤ WAYS TO CONDUCT CONVERSATIONS EASILY WITH PEOPLE OF OTHER CULTURES

➤ DIFFERENCES IN BODY LANGUAGE AMONG VARIOUS CULTURES

➤ REGIONAL DIFFERENCES AMONG AMERICANS

This section discusses international customs and looks at the perceptions other people in the world have of Americans. It is important to understand how others view us before we look at how different we are from others. This module also will discuss interacting with international visitors coming to America, rather than dealing with the intricacies of foreign travel.

In reality, we in America are truly a melting pot of people from all over the world, and it is difficult to typecast who "we" are. However, people from other nations do have a notion of what Americans are like. This may come as a surprise, but Americans are thought to be happy, friendly, gregarious, outgoing, and generous. Americans are also thought to be loud, obnoxious, egocentric, impolite, fast, and rich. These perceptions are a result of the many films that have captured "life in America" and spread throughout the world. Keeping these thoughts in mind can help us when we interact with international visitors or when we visit other countries.

©EyeWire

International Visitors

Note that people from other countries were referred to as "visitors." Sherri Ferris reminds us that "Whether you're doing business abroad, vacationing in a distant land or simply welcoming guests from another culture, with a little research and preparation, accompanied with some sensitivity skills training, you can make a lasting and favorable impression instead of a disastrous one. You never get another chance to make a first impression! In fact, wipe out the word 'foreign' or 'foreigner' from your vocabulary because in the dictionary it means 'alien' or 'not belonging.' Better to refer to others as 'visitors or guests.'[8]

When you are a visitor in another country, the best thing to do is follow the old adage "When in Rome, do as the Romans do." Observe what is going on around you. Be sensitive to how people live their lives. Try to fit in without being too conspicuous. Be aware of the perceptions others have of us, and try to dispel the negative images. Talk more softly, be considerate and polite to others, move at a slower pace, and travel within modest means.

In general, try not to be too friendly too soon. Do not call people by their first names until they have given their permission. Resist the American behavior of quick informality. Other countries take longer than Americans to "warm up" to people, and they generally observe a greater formality. Be patient when building trust in new relationships. For instance, when meeting someone from Great Britain for the first time, you would not ask what his or her occupation is.

In most parts of the United States, people generally are not very generous with the terms "please" and "thank you." Additionally the terms "yes, sir" and "yes, ma'am" are rarely heard except in the southern states. Because of this neglectful habit, Americans are generally perceived as being impolite. Most people from other countries use "please" and "thank you" generously, as well as the courtesy titles. When entertaining people from other countries, you may want to sprinkle these terms into your vocabulary.

"Before receiving or meeting an honored guest from abroad, prepare by researching such data such as their population, ethnic and religious composition, official languages, geography, especially the capital and major cities, their government structure, national leaders and political parties. Not only will you appear informed but your guest will be complimented because you took the time to learn something about him or her," advises Sherri Ferris.[8]

©DigitalVision

In almost every culture, it is courteous to stand when you are introduced to another person. Shaking hands is an American way of meeting people, and visitors usually expect it. When meeting Asian people, a handshake might be accompanied by a slight bow or nod of the head.

Treat international guests as very important people in your life. Escort them to a seat, or at least indicate where they might be seated. Seat them where you would seat a special guest. If there is a head table, seat them there. If you are being seated at a round table, place then next to someone of importance who also will be able to assist them if they have questions. Find the most comfortable seat if possible. Show them you really care about their well-being.

If an international visitor hands you a business card at your first business meeting, accept it with both hands, and scan it immediately for the vital information. Then lay the card in front of you on the table. Others may consider it demeaning if you put their card directly into your pocket without looking at it first; it may also be considered impolite to write on someone's card in his or her presence.

Humility is a trait that does not seem to be rewarded much in America, but it is highly regarded in many countries, especially in Asia. If a person from an Asian country gives you a compliment, it is polite to deny it graciously since modesty is highly valued there.

Conversing with International Visitors

Avoid sensitive subjects as topics of conversation, including religion and politics. From your research, you can identify safe subjects for topics of conversation. Acknowledge a national attraction. Sports is always a safe topic. Mention someone from their country who did well in the Olympics or a winning soccer team.

Speak slowly and enunciate each syllable. Those who have learned English from a textbook or in a classroom environment generally comprehend individual words. Saying "I do not know" in four clear syllables is easier to comprehend than "I don't know" and certain-ly better than, "I dunno." People erroneously increase the volume of their voice when speaking to individuals who do not understand the language. Volume does not increase comprehension. Our visitors typically are not hard of hearing; you just need to speak more slowly and enunciate each word.

Avoid jargon when communicating with international visitors. Try to avoid American slang, which has become so much a part of our daily lives. For instance, imagine how a person learning English would comprehend this monologue: "I'll be doggoned. He drives me nuts. Who gives a darned if we spend an hour grazing this buffet table? Tell him to bug off. I'll give him a piece of my mind when I return." Could you explain how a dog could be gone or how you could drive to become a type of nut? How can you provide a section of your mind to another person?

Body Language. Observe your international visitors to understand differences in their body language. Touching others and distance between people are two practices that vary in other cultures. Keep in mind that Americans are generally fond of shaking hands, touching, nudging, backslapping, embracing, and holding hands; this all is part of our everyday life. However, some cultures may be shocked at seeing this; other cultures will see it as acceptable. When Italians greet their friends, for instance, they routinely kiss briefly on each cheek (left cheeks together first, followed by right cheeks). Even men embrace each other in this fashion. Watch your visitors to see what is typical behavior for them.

Nonverbal interaction cues are extremely important. "Yes" or an affirmative nod often means "Yes, I hear you" in Asian cultures, not "Yes, I agree." Looking at the interaction through American eyes, you might think you just came to agreement on something important. Understand that by avoiding the word "no," some Asians believe they can prevent disharmony, and harmony is a cherished value in their culture.

Regional differences within the United States. We have discussed cultural differences with international visitors to America, but there are also subtle differences among those who live in the United States. There are regional differences as well as cultural differences among the American people.

Living in California my whole life, yet traveling extensively throughout the United States and the world, I am aware that others perceive Californians to be tanned, radical, fast paced, and dressed casually. This may be true, but most likely it is not. When entertaining visitors from the Midwest or East Coast, I know that their business attire likely will be dressier than California typical business attire. When entertaining visitors from Texas, in a respectful way, I try to use "sir" and "ma'am" when appropriate.

RECAP OF KEY CONCEPTS

- People in other countries perceive Americans as happy, friendly, gregarious, outgoing, and generous; they also perceive Americans as loud, obnoxious, egocentric, impolite, fast, and rich.
- When entertaining international visitors, think about what their perceptions are, and adjust your behavior accordingly.
- Research your visitor's country to identify safe topics of conversation (such as sports heroes and national attractions).
- When talking to an international visitor, speak slowly and enunciate.

Other DOs and DON'Ts

➤ **O**BTAINING CLARITY ON OFFICE HOLIDAY ACTIVITIES
➤ **A**PPROPRIATE WAYS TO DISPLAY THE **A**MERICAN FLAG

 his final section will focus on some miscellaneous topics concerning etiquette in the business environment.

Holidays and Gift Giving

Find out as early as possible about office culture so you are not embarrassed or make a social blunder. Ask "What goes on around here at Halloween?" "Do people exchange gifts here during the holidays?" Ask people at all levels; ask assistants, ask your peers, ask your boss.

ON THE SCENE

I asked my new assistant what everyone did during Halloween. She said, "Oh, we've never done much in the past." Well, Halloween arrived, and I was about the only one not dressed in costume. Later I realized she was rather shy and did not enjoy dressing up for Halloween. She had indicated her personal preference without revealing the actual office custom.

Birthdays

courtesy of ©PhotoDisc, Inc.

Birthdays can be touchy, but no matter who you are or how old you are, you probably like being remembered in some way on your birthday. Shy people might prefer discreet recognition, such as a simple card. Other people might enjoy being taken to lunch. Gifts are probably not as appropriate as a special lunch and a card.

Gift giving can be problematic. A gift can make others feel uncomfortable. It infers that they need to give a gift back to you at an appropriate time. Many offices have worked out a system so that no one is uncomfortable. For example, contribution of "birthday money" can be pooled for acknowledging birthdays as a group.

ON THE SCENE

I worked at one college where an enthusiastic assistant loved birthdays. She collected $5 of "birthday money" from everybody once a year. One day each month, everyone gathered and celebrated the people who had birthdays that month. We all shared a piece of the birthday cake. A card for each individual had been signed by the whole team. This was a nice way to fairly celebrate everyone's birthday.

Flag Ceremonies

The flag of the United States of America has a certain ritual as to placement, height on the flagpole, and care. The following guidelines are taken directly from *The Federal Flag Code* - (Public Law 94-344, July 7, 1976).

It is the universal custom to display the flag only from sunrise to sunset on buildings and on stationary flagstaffs in the open. However, when a patriotic effect is desired, the flag may be displayed twenty-four hours a day if properly illuminated during the hours of darkness.

When displayed either horizontally or vertically against a wall, the union should be uppermost and to the flag's own right, that is, to the observer's left. When displayed in a window, the flag should be displayed in the same way, with the union or blue field to the left of the observer in the street.

No other flag or pennant should be placed above, or, if on the same level, to the right of the flag of the United States of America, except during church services conducted by naval chaplains at sea, when the church pennant may be flown above the flag during church services for the personnel of the Navy.

No person shall display the flag of the United Nations or any other national or international flag equal, above, or in a position of superior prominence or honor to, or in place of, the flag of the United States at any place within the United States or any Territory or possession thereof; Provided, that nothing in this section shall make unlawful the continuance of the practice heretofore followed of displaying the flag of the United Nations in a position of superior prominence or honor, and other national flags in positions of equal prominence or honor, with that of the flag of the United States at the headquarters of the United Nations.

courtesy of ©PhotoDisc, Inc.

When flags of States, cities, or localities, or pennants of societies are flown on the same halyard with the flag of the United States, the latter should always be at the peak.

When the flags are flown from adjacent staffs, the flag of the United States should be hoisted first and lowered last. No such flag or pennant may be placed above the flag of the United States or to the United States flag's right.

The flag of the United States of America, when it is displayed with another flag against a wall from crossed staffs, should be on the right, the flag's own right, and its staff should be in front of the staff of the other flag.

The flag of the United States of America should be at the center and at the highest point of the group when a number of flags of States or localities or pennants of societies are grouped and displayed from staffs.

When flags of two or more nations are displayed, they are to be flown from separate staffs of the same height. The flags should be of approximately equal size. International usage forbids the display of the flag of one nation above that of another nation in time of peace.

When used on a speaker's platform, the flag, if displayed flat, should be displayed above and behind the speaker. When displayed from a staff in a church or public auditorium, the flag of the United States of America should hold the position of superior prominence, in advance of the audience, and in the position of honor at the clergyman's or speaker's right as he faces the audience. Any other flag so displayed should be placed on the left of the clergyman or speaker or the right of the audience.

Half-Staff

The flag, when flown at half-staff, should be first hoisted to the peak for an instant and then lowered to the half-staff position. The flag should be again raised to the peak before it is lowered for the day. On Memorial Day the flag should be displayed at half-staff until noon only, then raised to the top of the staff. By order of the President, the flag shall be flown at half-staff upon the death of principal figures of the United States Government and the Governor of the State, territory, or possession, as a mark of respect to their memory. In the event of the death of other officials or foreign dignitaries, the flag is to be displayed at half-staff according to Presidential instructions or orders, or in accordance with recognized customs or practices not inconsistent with law. In the event of the death of a present or former official of the government of any State, territory, or possession of the United States, the Governor of that State, territory, or possession may proclaim that the National flag shall be flown at half-staff.

Note: the U.S. flag should always be on its own right in relation to other flags on adjacent staffs — to the left of the observer.

RECAP OF KEY CONCEPTS

- Identify the customs of your work environment regarding holidays and birthdays; know the office culture.
- The U.S. flag should be displayed only from sunrise to sunset on buildings and on stationary flagstaffs in the open; it may be displayed 24 hours a day if properly illuminated during the hours of darkness.

Case Studies

The case studies presented here provide you with material for group discussion, individual written exercises, or whatever works best in your instructional setting.

1. A special guest will be visiting the company at which you work — Best Telecom Industries. You have been asked to give the guest a tour, which will involve introducing her to various key people in the company. Plan how you will introduce your guest to each of the individuals along your tour. Here are the particulars on your guest and the people you will meet.

    Guest: Helen Rudee is the local county supervisor. She is a mature woman who has been involved in politics at all levels. She is a rather sophisticated person and very comfortable to be around.

    The people on your tour route to whom you will introduce her are as follows:
    Sean Green, supervisor of quality control, middle management, is a new hire to the company.
    Jill Brown, director of human relations, upper management, a fun person, knows everyone in the company, puts together the company barbecue every summer.
    Bob Bentley, head custodian, plays on a city league soccer team.
    Li Li, administrative assistant to the president/CEO, is shy, received a company award last year for community service.
    Jesus Gonzalez, President/CEO, formed the company only five years ago, has been extremely successful.

2. An international guest is arriving to visit your company. His name is Vladmir Posovich, and he is coming from the city of Cherkassy in the Ukraine. Your boss has asked you to research the Ukraine and its customs. Identify some helpful facts about the country, local customs, and courtesies. Identify safe topics for conversation as well as topics to avoid.

3. You have been asked to arrange a dinner meeting for seven visitors to your company. You have met some of the visitors, but not all of them. Your boss will not be able to attend because she has a prior engagement. You are in charge of the dinner. What details do you need to consider so you will have everything under control during the dinner?

4. There is a serious concern at your company about public relations. A slow response rate makes printed materials almost out of date by the time they are printed. You have been asked to organize and facilitate a meeting about this problem. Consider all the people who should attend the meeting and why you would request their attendance. Design the invitation and agenda.

Online Resources

International Business Etiquette
http://www.econ.state.or.us/OregonTrade/
International Division of the Oregon Economic & Community
Development Department with links to international business etiquette.

Job Interview Etiquette
http://www.fordham.edu/cpp/interviewetiquette.htm
This link is provided through the Fordham University Office of Career
Planning and Placement and discusses appropriate etiquette during a job
interview.

Online Column on Etiquette
http://www.mustudent.muohio.edu/Vol124a/no16/op-ed/pers1.html
This column on etiquette is written in "The Miami Student," an online
edition of the campus newspaper for Miami University, Oxford, Ohio.

Protocol Tips
http://www.protocolprofessionals.com/
An international relations consulting firm with links to "Protocol Tips."

Article by Etiquette Expert
http://cnnfn.cnn.com/mybusiness/9606/18/
A web article by Letitia Baldrige, Etiquette Expert, in the CNNfn—the
Financial Network.

Note: These Web sites were operational at the time of printing.
However, since the Web is ever-changing, specific URLs can change
or expire very quickly. If you are unable to access these sites, use the
following keywords to conduct an Internet search:

Business Etiquette	International customs
Business Protocol	International relations
Corporate Culture	People skills
Corporate dress	Dining etiquette
Job interview etiquette	Table manners

Endnotes

[1] Letitia Baldrige, an etiquette expert who served on staff for Jacqueline Kennedy in the White House.

[2] The US Office of Consumer Affairs published a study that identified the actual costs of substandard business etiquette.

[3] Carnegie, Dale. *How to Win Friends and Influence People*. Simon & Schuster, 1982.

[4] Gabor, Don. *How to Start a Conversation and Make Friends.* Simon & Schuster, 1983.

[5] Phillips, Grenville W. *The Administration and Conduct of Corporate Meetings.* The University of the West Indies Press, 1996.

[6] Southworth, William Dixon. *The Art of Successful Meetings.* McGraw Hill College Division, 1997.

[7] Nelson, Robert. *Better Business Meetings.* Irwin Professional Pub. 1994.

[8] Ferris, Sherri. GLOBAL VILLAGE ETIQUETTE: How to avoid offending international guests Protocol International Internet site: http://www.drcomputer.com/protocol/etiquett.htm

Post-Assessment Activity

Circle the response below that best describes your current belief. You may recognize these questions from the PRE-ASSESSMENT. Do not review your original answers. Complete this page, and then compare with your original answers to see how much you have grown. For those questions that show no growth, you may want to go back and review those topics. Do not be discouraged as changing life-long habits is not an overnight accomplishment. Keep this text for the future and refer to it often!

Never	Almost Never	Seldom	Sometimes	Usually	Almost Always	Always
1	2	3	4	5	6	7

THERE ARE NO RIGHT OR WRONG ANSWERS. There also is no time limit, but you should work as rapidly as possible. Please respond to every item on the list.

Items: ***Never   Always***

1. I know most rules of etiquette, and I know when I am purposely breaking a rule.   1 2 3 4 5 6 7

2. I am comfortable walking down a sidewalk with my colleagues—both men and women.   1 2 3 4 5 6 7

3. I feel as though my clothes are "business professional" for my particular work environment.   1 2 3 4 5 6 7

4. I am very comfortable with small talk at a business function.   1 2 3 4 5 6 7

5. I am comfortable introducing people, especially those at work.   1 2 3 4 5 6 7

6. I am pleased to shake hands with whomever I am being introduced—men and women, old and young.   1 2 3 4 5 6 7

7. I am familiar with what rules of etiquette to follow at the workplace.   1 2 3 4 5 6 7

8. I know how to organize and facilitate a meeting so that I respect everyone in attendance.   1 2 3 4 5 6 7

9. I am very comfortable eating a meal in the presence of higher-level employees at work.   1 2 3 4 5 6 7

10. I am very comfortable when it comes time to decide who is to pay the restaurant tab.   1 2 3 4 5 6 7

11. I am aware of the misperceptions that international visitors may have of Americans, which then helps me adjust my behavior.   1 2 3 4 5 6 7

12. I am comfortable speaking with international visitors.   1 2 3 4 5 6 7

13. I am comfortable with my knowledge of how to display the U.S. flag.   1 2 3 4 5 6 7

Notes

Notes

Notes

Notes